PREDATOR VS PREY

Polar Bear Vs Seal

Mary Meinking

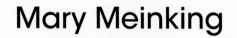

www.raintreepublishers.co.uk
Visit our website to find out
more information about
Raintree books.

To order:
☎ Phone 0845 6044371
🖨 Fax +44 (0) 1865 312263
💻 Email myorders@raintreepublishers.co.uk

Customers from outside the UK please telephone +44 1865 312262

Raintree is an imprint of Capstone Global Library Limited,
a company incorporated in England and Wales having its
registered office at 7 Pilgrim Street, London, EC4V 6LB –
Registered company number: 6695582

Edited by Rebecca Rissman, Dan Nunn,
    and Catherine Veitch
Designed by Joanna Hinton Malivoire
Levelling by Jeanne Clidas
Picture research by Hannah Taylor
Production by Victoria Fitzgerald
Originated by Capstone Global Library
Printed and bound in China by CTPS

ISBN 978 1 406 21869 5
14 13 12 11 10
10 9 8 7 6 5 4 3 2 1

British Library Cataloguing in Publication Data
Meinking, Mary.
Polar bear vs seal. -- (Predator vs prey)
591.5'3-dc22
A full catalogue record for this book is available from the
British Library.

Acknowledgements
We would like to thank the following for permission
to reproduce photographs: Alamy Images p. 15 (© Steven
J. Kazlowski); Corbis pp. 5 (Paul Souders), 9 (Paul Souders),
20 (Radius Images/ Chris Hendrickson), 29 (San Francisco
Chronicle/ Kat Wade); FLPA pp. 7 (Minden Pictures/ Tui De
Roy), 11 (Flip Nicklin/Minden Pictures), 18 (Imagebroker),
21 (Sunset); Getty Images pp. 10 (Paul Nicklen), 19
(National Geographic), 23 (National Geographic), 24
(National Geographic/ Paul Nicklen); istockphoto p. 6 (©
VisualCommunications); naturepl pp. 12 (Steven Kazlowski),
17 (Andy Rouse); Photolibrary pp. 8 (Peter Arnold Images/
Steven Kazlowski), 13 (Peter Arnold Images/ S.J. Krasemann),
14 (Peter Arnold Images/ Steven Kazlowski), 16 (Peter
Arnold Images/ Steven Kazlowski), 25 (Alaskastock/ Steven
Kazlowski), 27 (Alaskastock), 28 (Alaskastock/ Steven
Kazlowski); Rex Features p. 22 (naturepl/ Mats Forsberg);
SeaPics.com p. 4 (Bryan & Cherry Alexander); Still Pics p. 26
(Peter Arnold/ Fred Bruemmer).

Cover photographs of a polar bear reproduced with
permission of Photolibrary (Alaskastock/ Steven Kazlowski),
and a ringed seal reproduced with permission of FLPA
(Minden Pictures/ Tui De Roy).

We would like to thank Michael Bright for his invaluable help
in the preparation of this book.

Every effort has been made to contact copyright holders of
material reproduced in this book. Any omissions will
be rectified in subsequent printings if notice is given to the
publisher.

Some words are shown in bold, **like this**. You can find
out what they mean by looking in the glossary.

Contents

Icy battle

Claws slash! Flippers splash! Two animals meet in an icy white battlefield. Here is the world's largest **carnivore** on land, the polar bear. It is up against a slippery challenger, the seal.

seal

polar bear

5

The competitors live in the icy **Arctic**. Both have strengths that will help them in this battle.

PREDATOR
polar bear

LENGTH: 3 metres

WEIGHT: 635 kilograms

SAME SIZE AS: a medium-sized car

Key

where polar bears and Arctic ringed seals live

PREY
Arctic ringed seal

LENGTH: 1.2 metres

WEIGHT: 52 kilograms

SAME SIZE AS: a large dog

Arctic

King of the north

Polar bears live alone. They cross the ice and snow and swim in the sea looking for food. They wander over 64 kilometres every day. That's further than 640 football pitches.

DID YOU KNOW?
Polar bears can be found a long way from the shore. Sometimes they float on big chunks of ice, like rafts.

Hold their breath

The seal swims under the ice like a fish. But it's a **mammal**. So it comes up for air every 8 to 15 minutes.

DID YOU KNOW?

Seals use their front claws to make air holes in the ice so they can breathe. Some holes go through nearly 2 metres of ice!

Who's hungry?

The polar bear is a **carnivore**, or meat eater. It often eats seals. The polar bear lies next to seal air holes. It waits for a seal to come up for air. If one appears, the polar bear grabs it. But it can be a long wait.

air hole

Polar bears can go for six days without eating!

Sneak attack

One morning the seal climbs onto the ice to lay in the sun. But it stays close to its air hole. The polar bear heads across the ice looking for **prey**. It sniffs the air. Soon it picks up the **scent,** or smell of a seal.

DID YOU KNOW?
A polar bear can smell a seal from one kilometre away. That's about 1,000 steps away!

The polar bear quietly slides into the icy water. Its long neck keeps its head out of the water when it swims. Then the polar bear crawls out onto the ice. It shakes itself off, like a dog.

DID YOU KNOW?

Polar bears are strong swimmers. They can swim up to 96 kilometres without stopping. That's as far as swimming a pool 384 times!

The polar bear follows the **scent** until it spots the seal. The polar bear looks for the best place to sneak up on the seal. Seals cannot see things that are far away very well.

DID YOU KNOW?

The biggest danger for Arctic seals is not the polar bear – it's **global warming**! Much of their icy home is melting as the weather gets warmer.

19

The polar bear gets down low and creeps slowly towards the seal. It is hard for the seal to see and hear the bear. The polar bear's white coat **blends** in with the snow and ice.

The polar bear has huge 30-centimetre-wide paws. These dinner plate-sized paws have fur on the bottom. This helps them sneak around quietly.

DID YOU KNOW?
Polar bears can run up to 40 kilometres an hour. That's as fast as a motor scooter!

When the polar bear is close, it **charges** at the seal. The seal sees the bear coming. It uses its front flippers to drag itself over the ice. It wriggles towards the water. The polar bear gets closer and closer until the seal reaches the water's edge.

The seal dives in. It shoots down deep like a **torpedo**. Its front flippers steer and its rear flippers push it through the water like a fish. The polar bear dives into the sea after the seal, but it can't go as deep as the seal.

And the winner is...

...the seal! Seals are better swimmers than polar bears. They can hold their breath for up to 45 minutes and dive down to 90 metres. That's as deep as a 30-storey building is tall!

Polar bears can only stay under water for two minutes.

What are the odds?

Polar bears catch **prey** once out of every 50 tries! They only catch a seal every four or five days. Polar bears need to eat lots of fat, or **blubber**, for energy. Seals have thick layers of blubber, which makes them great meals!

Glossary

Arctic area around the North Pole

blend when things mix together so that you cannot tell them apart

blubber thick layer of fat under animals' skin

carnivore animal that eats meat

charge rush or attack

global warming rise in temperature of the surface of the Earth, including the land, sea, and air. This causes weather changes around the world.

mammal warm-blooded animal that feeds its young milk

predator animal that hunts other animals

prey animal that is hunted by other animals for food

scent smell given off by an animal

torpedo explosive missile shot underwater at a target

Find out more

Books

Animal Top Tens: The Polar Regions' Most Amazing Animals, Anita Ganeri (Raintree, 2008)

Animals in Danger: Polar Bears (Ticktock Media, 2006)

Face to Face with Polar Bears, Norbert Rosing (National Geographic Society, 2009)

Websites

http://gowild.wwf.org.uk/gowild/amazing_animals/
On this website you can find out more about polar bears and other amazing animals and watch videos of them in the wild.

http://kids.nationalgeographic.com/Animals/CreatureFeature/Polar-bear
Learn more about polar bears on this website.

http://www.ecokids.ca/pub/eco_info/topics/field_guide/mammals/ringed_seal.cfm
Find out more about the Ringed seal on this website.

Index